T0146618

Never Ending Speed Bumps

Never Ending Speed Bumps

My God Is More Than Enough

BAILEY BRUNER

NEVER ENDING SPEED BUMPS
MY GOD IS MORE THAN ENOUGH

iUniverse books may be ordered through booksellers or by contacting:

iUniverse
1663 Liberty Drive
Bloomington, IN 47403
www.iuniverse.com
1-800-Authors (1-800-288-4677)

ISBN: 978-1-5320-6525-5 (sc)
ISBN: 978-1-5320-6526-2 (e)

Library of Congress Control Number: 2018914881

Print information available on the last page.

iUniverse rev. date: 12/17/2018

CHAPTER 1

Background Check

Backwoods, dirt road driveways, and the closest neighbor to you is a mile down the road is what I see when I describe home. Snow Camp, a little old city in North Carolina is where I went to school, how I met my best friends, and was developed into who I am today. When I was growing up in that town, the only sport that existed in my eyes was football. When I was at E.M. Holt Elementary, my buddies and I would play football during recess. And you know, of course, at the beginning of the game everyone wants to agree on "no tackling" but at the end of recess we come back to class with grass stains on our jeans and bumps and bruises all over our body. Some of the many things that I love about football are: getting dirty and getting cuts and getting bruises. I thought that was a sign to show people that you were tough and to let people know not to mess with you. Even when I was at home, I would beg my dad over and over again to play catch with me before dinner; and, nine times out of ten he would go throw the football with me. We would go back and forth on who would be the quarterback and who would be the receiver. I would run my dad to death; but even though he would get tired, he would see the smile he put on my face and would continue on running Hail Marys for me until I either got tired myself or hungry, whichever came first.

Fifth grade rolled around and life, in general, was going well. Nothing to worry about right?

As I was waiting to be picked up from my mom at school, I was so happy to tell my mom I had gotten a good grade on my test-when I got a good grade in school we had to frame it because something like that came once in a blue moon. I hopped in the car and tried to sort everything in my head into what I was going to say. I could tell by my mom's face she wasn't happy. The happiness that was radiating off of me dwindled down. Her phone rang and it was my dad. As we got farther and farther into our drive home, they were getting angrier at each other, biting each other's head off left and right, and I had no clue what was going on. We pulled in our driveway and I had totally forgotten the good news I was going to tell my mom, but at this point it didn't really matter to me; all that mattered to me was what was going on between my mom and dad. I went to my room and told my parents I was doing my homework. But, I was really at my door trying to listen in on their conversation. I wasn't sure exactly what being "laid off" meant; but that's the only thing I heard being repeated over and over again. That morning everything was calm, they gave each other a hug and kiss like they do every morning and now it seemed like everything went into a total three hundred -sixty degree turn. When I came home from school not saying a word to my parents, but I wanted so badly to ask them what all happened the day before. Sure enough, after my dad came home, they both came in my room. That was when I knew they were going to tell me everything. I had been guessing all day what they could have been talking about, ranging from a divorce, death, and moving. Believe it or not, I was actually correct on one of my guesses. We had to move. My mom explained how she had been laid off at her job and we would have to move for her to find another job. I didn't know that "moving" meant moving to another state.

That was one the most difficult and most uncomfortable things I've done. It meant leaving my whole childhood and basically my whole life behind in North Carolina. Meeting new friends was going to be a difficult thing for me to do. I would be going to a middle school that had double the amount of students my old school had. I knew that the most difficult part of transitioning was going to be leaving family and friends. I had no clue what I was going to do. Everybody in South Carolina seemed like a different breed of people to me. Everybody seemed like that they were from up North and that they were huge Steelers fans. One thing I could never wrap my head around was that people in my neighborhood would hang up banners and flags around their house that said "It's Steeler Country." I just learned to go with the flow and not question those people and their thinking process.

It's like being a Yankees fan and growing up in Boston. However, to make a long story short, I'd have to admit that making friends in Myrtle Beach was pretty difficult.They weren't the nicest people to talk to at times. Like for example, for me it wasn't easy to make friends because I wasn't a very outgoing person. Although I have to admit that I did enjoy my time living in Myrtle Beach, my neighbors were always a blast to be around.

Every Friday night my parents and I would go to their house and hangout at their house watching a game of some sort on tv and basically having a good time while telling stories about how our week went. Butch and Gal, were a couple whose house we would go to and I would always look forward to going to their house because I knew if I was there I had reached the end of the week and I could relax. Around a year later, my cousins, Kayla and Ceria decided that they were going to move to Myrtle Beach as well and I was so excited to hear that news because it only made it easier for me to go through school knowing I knew someone there, and the best part is that they were my cousins. Another cool part about my cousins moving to South Carolina is that they lived literally next door from me, our backyard connected to each other that led to a big pond in both of our backyards. The one thing I can always remember, while me and my cousin's were fishing one afternoon is that while Kayla was fishing she somehow hooked a bird that was flying in the sky. Don't ask me how she did it but she made the impossible, possible. Also riding bikes with Kayla and Ceria after school, we would hang out at our community park until it would get dark. These special moments that we had with each other is what made it possible for me to actually enjoy living in a new state, nothing like family that you can always come to at the end of the day and make life seem so much better. Like I said earlier it was still difficult to make friends outside of family, nevertheless playing sports. Making the middle school football was tough for me to do.

I was cut from the team before my seventh grade year. It hurt me a lot to be cut. It was like someone had just punched me in the gut. After playing football growing up, then moving to a new school, and then being cut was embarrassing and disheartening. I remember crying all that night. I didn't even eat dinner- that's how angry and upset I was. I was thinking about not trying out the next year because it put a bad taste in my mouth when I began thinking that I wasn't good enough to play. I was thinking about trying something new and change things up a little next year. In that same year, I played in my church football league. That year, I played for one of the best coaches I was ever coached by, Coach Ron. He was the best motivator I have ever met. Of course the team's name was the Steelers and his favorite team was the Pittsburgh Steelers. So I put two and two together. That season I played the weird combination of center and linebacker. I'll never forget that team. The first time I ever got a pick six against the Colts gave me the best feeling I've ever had up until that point in my life. Coach Ron wanted me to play quarterback for him the next season, however, I had no clue what I wanted to do next year, as far as playing for the Steelers or my middle school team. As my seventh grade summer was ending and the start of a new football season was about to begin, I was uneasy about trying out again for the middle school team. One morning as my dad was taking me to school we talked about the last year and he was questioning me on why I didn't want to play football anymore; and of course I said "It's because I'm no good at football." I'll never forget about what my dad told me that morning, he said "why did you even play football?" I was a little confused by what he meant, so he explained that I have to go back mentally to when I first played pee-wee football and the first time I ever put on shoulder pads, how I had to have help buckling my helmet for the first time. He explained, "Get that same excitement back that you had when you were a little boy to where you wanted to hit everybody in your path even your own teammates at times." My dad always knew what to say at the right time and it made my decision clear that I wanted to tryout once again for my middle school team.

I was underrated-that's for sure. I wasn't the biggest or fastest person on the team, but I'm sure that I had the most heart and grit. There were three days of tryouts.One day was specific position drills. Then, the next day there was your normal forty yard dash, vertical jump test, and shuffle drills- just like the NFL combine. On the last day of tryouts you were able to finally see if you made the team. On that last day all the guys were just sitting in the gym with the coaches sitting at a table in front of us getting their final paperwork in... I wasn't talking with anyone. I was so ready to see what the results were and I had no time for small talk with the other guys. One by one, the coaches called a player down and that's when he would find out if he had made the team or not. Well, when my name was finally called my heart was beating out of my chest because I was so nervous. The first thing that the coach asked me was "are you ready to be a part of this program?" And because I was so nervous, I accidentally said "no" instead of "yes." He looked at me funny, like he was not ready for that response, but quickly I corrected myself and said, "Yes." That put a smile on his face. At that point on I felt like I was on top of the world, like someone had given me a new car, like a dream come true.

As I said I wasn't the biggest, so I was one of the linebackers that were overlooked a lot during practice, until there was finally a chance for me to make something happen. My dad always told me to play "a hundred and ten percent every play" and to play "like it's your last play." Well when coach called my name to play linebacker in a game, I was looking at in the back field was the quarterback, of course, but also a 230 pound fullback that would be coming in my direction. I said a mini prayer before the play started. The quarterback hiked the ball and he handed it to the fullback. He cut to the outside, I had a perfect "one on one" tackle opportunity. I reached out and went for the legs of that bowling ball. He went down, but he got right back up as I was still collecting up the rest of my body that was still on the field. Even though I had gotten a concussion that was a very proud moment for me; because I had tackled one of the biggest guys on the opposing team. One night after I had gotten home from football practice, I quickly ate dinner and got ready for bed.

As I was brushing my teeth, my mom popped her head in the doorway and said "Hey Bay let me know when you're done in here, I have to asked you a quick question."

A little confused on what she wanted to talk about, not knowing if I did something wrong in school or something less complex than that. Laying in my bed felt like I was laying on a cloud, and after a long day like I had I wasn't really in the mood to talk but shortly after I went into my bed, she came walking through my door.

She sat down at the edge of my bed and asked me "Well, me and your dad have another job opportunity."

Not saying a word, yet but thinking like I was going to cry, believing I might have to move to another state and to attempt meeting new people again. Then, she went on to explain that the job opportunity is back in my home state of North Carolina. I was very excited, knowing I can go to school with my friends again that I haven't seen in years. My mom asked me if I would be okay with moving back, and before she told me to sleep on the idea, I already agreed to moving back. Once my decision was made, we began packing. After three years of living at the beach, we finally moved back to North Carolina right after my football season was over. Jobs were hard to keep and we needed our family the most.

Coming back home was a little strange just because of the simple fact that I hadn't seen my home town in a few years and things had changed. Local malls, restaurants, and even some old friends were just gone and out of my life. Although, the transition back wasn't as bad as leaving had been. I was able to see my family more often again and I even made some new friends in eighth grade. I wasn't able to play football at my new middle school because I just moved back right after their season was over. My next shot at playing football was going to be in high school. As a middle school student-athlete I never realized that there were summer workouts for high school until my dad informed me one day that there were. After a couple weeks of it, I quickly realized that I hated everything about it. (So did my mom as she had to smell me every day after summer workouts.) Those ninety degree summer days were brutal and I counted down the days to when it was over. As a freshman I was obviously a little nervous and I didn't know what to expect from the team.

During the summer we would have days where we would just lift and watch some film. I knew I wasn't the biggest guy in the room. When I saw the varsity team lifting they looked like giants compared to me. There were guys benching two hundred pounds for warm ups and maxing out on squat at four hundred plus pounds. At times, they made me question myself and wonder why in the world I was even in there. As the 2013-14 season came, we looked like a sharp team that was hunting for a state championship ring. I played running back and receiver my freshman year on the junior varsity team- and we actually had a better record that the varsity team. But, the varsity still went to playoffs because that year our team was stacked with athletes. Due to being a freshman, I didn't really touch the field that much that year. The most excitement I had was scoring my first high school touchdown. I told myself after our last game that next season was going to be so much more different. I was going to prove myself to the coaches that I could not just play but also could start every game.

CHAPTER 2

Proverbs 3:4-6

After my first semester ended and I was heading into my second semester of freshman year, I wanted to still train for next football season. I knew that two of my buddies, Joe Joe, and Austin were lifting and training after school, so I got into contact with them and asked if I could join them and coach Bishop, who was also our defensive backs coach at the time. Going and attending these workouts is what made me begin talking to coach. After school we would go to the weight room and train non-stop, following film right after. I also met some of my closest friends who were also training for football. Austin Johnson, Austin McCleandon, and coach Bishop were three guys that I met throughout the remaining of the semester during workouts and I'm so happy that I did because they are forever my life long friends. I'll never forget the first time coach Bishop made us do "Fun Friday."

Don't let the name fool you because there was nothing fun about it, it was a series of lifts, conditioning, basically like a "High Intensity Training" concept. I can't tell you how many times that my legs were not opporatable after each session and how I felt like I needed to throw up. Although somehow I managed to get up the next day and was able to function. All I was wishing at the time was I hope it would all pay off next football season. It was the summer of 2014 and summer football workouts were starting back up. I promised myself that was going to be better and stronger than I was the previous year and I wasn't going to let anything stop me from getting to that goal. I would bust my tail at everything, making sure I would do an extra rep and making it known for the coaches that I wanted to play. We would run sprints, run up and down the bleachers, and even perform bear crawls in the sand.

One afternoon after we just finished practice and doing our sprints, I felt a sensation in my neck to the point where it was throbbing, something I had never felt before. If I could describe it I would say that it felt like my actual heart beating through my neck. I got dressed and I left the locker room still wondering about my neck and as I got into my car I looked in my rear view mirror to see if my neck looked weird or maybe bigger which it was none of those things. I shook it off and tried to ignore it and gave myself a little pep talk to convince myself nothing was wrong.

We had two weeks total of vacation time that summer and those weeks were spread out through July. For my final week of summer vacation, I was headed to Myrtle Beach with my family to visit some old friends that we hadn't seen in a long time. Even though we were on vacation, I still made time to go on jogs on the beach to stay conditioned, trying to make a self goal by jogging from pier to pier. I wanted to have fun, but I also knew that it was very important for me to stay in shape for football. Throughout the week my family and I went to the beach, visited some old friends, and even tried the banana boat ride- because why not? Friday got closer and closer and it was finally the day we had to leave and go back home for the rest of the summer. When we got closer to home we decided we all wanted to eat out one last time for our vacation.

It was the first time my mom ever noticed... it was the first time that she ever noticed the big lump on the front side of my neck.

I was sitting across from both of my parents. My mom noticed that every time I swallowed my food that there was some kind of mass on my neck that kept moving as well. I have to admit I was kind of nervous. I could see it on my parents' face that they were a little uneasy too. After we ate our dinner we all made the decision to go to the hospital to get it checked out. My mom had a knot in her throat, but it was not cancerous or anything, but she had to get her whole thyroid removed. She explained to me that it was nothing to worry about and I shouldn't overreact to this situation. So, when she saw this lump on my neck she kinda put two and two together. After waiting for countless hours in the waiting room for someone, just anybody, to say Bailey, we were finally called to go back. (Apparently we picked the wrong day to go to the emergency room because we didn't leave the hospital until three in the morning) We got back to what I call "the second waiting room" which means we still were waiting on the doctor to come through the door. Then, he finally did.

As he was examining me and pushing on my throat, it felt extremely uncomfortable. Every time he touched and put pressure in that area of the mass, I about jumped off the examining table and hit him- it was that painful. He told us that the size of the mass was the size of a golf ball and that it was still growing. He also mentioned two possibilities for what it could be. It could just be a mass that could easily be taken care of or it could be cancer. Never in my life had I ever thought of myself having cancer; it felt like a dream that went horribly wrong. Of course, my parents told me not worry about it and that I would be fine, "It's just a possibility..." they said, "...nothing could go wrong." The first visit which was Sunday night we were at the hospital and on Wednesday of that same week we got a phone call. It was my doctor calling and was wondering how I was doing. Even he was worried and he mentioned how he never seen anything like it before. We were scheduled to see an Endocrinologist- or to shorten it up a little, an ear, nose, and throat doctor- later on in the month to get more lab work done and to finally figure out what this mass on my neck was.

Soon enough it was that time to go back to the doctor's office and to find out what was going on. At the time my mom was only with me, because my dad was at work. Usually you never see a doctor show any emotion while on duty. They just stay calm and collected but, he walked into our room and I could see from the look of his face that he was upset. It looked like he had been crying before he even came into the room. It turned out that he had to tell a fourteen year old boy that he had been diagnosed with cancer...that fourteen year old boy was me. That doctor was the same doctor who's dad operated on my mom's thyroid when she was younger; so, we knew him pretty well. When he was telling me I had cancer it was like telling a family member that they were diagnosed. I tried to hold back the tears because my mom was sitting right next to me and I didn't want her to know I was scared. I just wanted to be strong at the time. Once my doctor told me the unpleasant news, he had to leave the room so he could regroup himself. His assistant was still in the room and she came up to me with a soft voice and asked me if I was okay. At that point I lost it. My eyes looked like a dam that had just burst. I felt so helpless at that point, wondering why God put this on a fourteen year boy like me, what had I done to deserve this? My mom came over immediately to comfort me and she told me "...not to worry, that everything was going to be okay" and that "God had a plan for me." I remember going home that night bawling my eyes out crying out to God, asking for forgiveness, saying I'm sorry a thousand times, and just wishing maybe. Just maybe it was just a bad dream.

The next day I didn't go to school, heck I didn't even come out of bed. It was Thursday and my football team was playing against one of our biggest rivals that night, Eastern Alamance High School. I wanted to go so badly and my mom thought it would be best for me just to stay home. Well, I didn't listen to her and I somehow managed to convince her to let me go. I didn't mention anything to the guys about what was going on with me because I didn't want them to worry about me. I tried my best to act like I was fine when I got to the game. Earlier that day I had to go run to the hospital to get some more lab work done so by the time I was at the game I wasn't feeling too hot. I got a weird tingling sensation in my face and I felt very weak, before the game started and as the team was warming up, I walked down to the field and said "hey" to all the coaches. As warm-ups ended, our head coach told all the guys to take a knee in the end zone and then he walked up to me and asked "Do you want to let them know?" At the time I said "sure," but really I wish I should have said "no." Not because I wanted to be mean or anything; it was just because it was right before a game and I felt like it was a wrong time to tell them. But going against my better judgment, I told them. I told them that what the doctors found was cancerous; but it was a curable cancer and I would be perfectly fine. I also said that "I'll get through it with no problem."

I tried acting normal while talking to the team, but I couldn't hold myself up very well and I had to lean against the field goal post to help me stand up. So convincing the guys that I was okay was a hard task to do. Many of my teammates came up and hugged me and told me that they would keep me in their prayers. That was one of the many reasons why I loved that group of guys; they were always there for support when I needed it.

One month later, after multiple doctor visits and blood work, my forearms were scarred and blistered from the multiple punctures with needles that were constantly piercing my skin. I felt so weak and helpless at the time. I felt like a lab rat going back and forth to the hospital every single day after school. Every day I would have to get full body scans and blood work done. My normal day consisted of being in the hospital for hours, in and out of rooms, and being tested for everything you could imagine. I had so many hospital bands I could have started a collection with all of them. The amount of radiation I had inside me was so great that I had to stay out of school for two weeks; and that definitely took a toll on my grades. I can honestly that the worst part of radiation was taking that dang horse pill. Already having a hard enough time with swallowing pills as it is. I had to swallow this radiation pill, it came in a lead container and the radiologist were wearing gloves to handle it. The nurses told me to swallowing the pill quickly so it doesn't stay on my tongue for a very long time, reasoning behind that is because it could soon start to deteriorate my taste buds. I tried so hard to swallow that pill and it would not go down, it was starting to become annoying but the young ladies in the room were very patient with me as they offered me to put it in some applesauce and even peanut butter but nothing was working. There was time where I almost swallowed the pill but my gagged reflexes kicked in and I spit it back up on the floor. So this process which was only supposed to take at most fifteen minutes, took an hour and a half. Luckily they had a back up pill for me and soon enough I was able to take that pill. The nurses in the room told me that once I got into my car I had to sit in the back seat on the opposite corner of where my mom was driving. They explained the reasoning for that was because the radiation had already kicked in and they wanted me to be as far away as possible from everyone. I had to be quarantined in my room during that two week period and if I wanted to do homework or even touch the TV remote I had to wear latex gloves. Since I couldn't be near my parents they had to put my food outside of my bedroom door and let me step outside to get it. My food isn't something you pick up from the grocery store. Everything I ate had to be organically made by hand. It was called a low iodine diet. When I say it was nasty, I mean I almost threw up or gagged every time I ate it. I couldn't have anything with iodine. I could only eat certain fruits and vegetables and I could have only five ounces of meat per day.

This obviously made it very difficult for me to eat at school, being that my food had to be microwaved because it was all hand made food. I didn't know what to do about lunch. I even thought about not eating lunch at all at school. I could see the frustration on my mother's face as she would become very upset of how I was going to be like every other student and eat at school again. This was the first moment on how my coach, Matthew Bishop became a friend and later on a brother to me, I told him my situation about eating at school and he immediately told me and my parents that I could eat in his classroom during my lunch period and he could heat up my food in the teachers' lounge. When he told us that, all you could see was pure happiness glowing on our faces. He even took his own money and bought me vegetables that I could throughout the day at school if I started to feel sick or weak.

A couple weeks went by as I continued to eat in his classroom, Austin Johnson one of my buddies started to join me as well. I don't know if he realizes this but it made my day when he came and ate with me during my lunch period. There was always two memories that stuck out to me the most that I will always remember. I remember for one lunch Austin had a bag of grapes that he had packed that day. As he started to eat them he had a weird look to his face every time he ate them. I asked him if they were bad but he said that they had a funny taste to them. At the time, he kept his lunch box in the same bag as his gym bag. He didn't realize until a few minutes later that his cologne leaked into his grapes and he had eaten every single one of them. That afternoon, even though we weren't playing at the time we still went to football practice and I glanced over at the sideline to find Austin hunched over the trash can puking up those nasty grapes. Speaking of the vegetables coach Bishop would get for me- it was half time during one of our home football games and standing on the sidelines made me pretty hungry. Austin and I were just about to pay for food at the concessions, but I quickly remembered I couldn't eat that food so I told him I had a better idea. e causally made our way up to coach Bishop's classroom and started going to town on all the vegetables that he had brought, as the halftime show was going on and the crowd still sitting in the bleachers me and Austin were chilling in his classroom probably having the most deepest and thoughtful conversations with each other while eating green bell peppers.

Although there were times that weren't so great and the radiation was taking a toll on my body. The longer I stayed in my room the more I could smell myself- and I'm not talking about body odor. The smell of the radiation started to pour out of my body and started to make me sick on a daily basis. For hours and nearly entire days I would throw up because of the smell of the radiation coming off of my body. Even when I slept through the night and started to sweat, I would wake up to my bed sheets being a different color due to the radiation. The only quick and easy way I could get rid of it was if I peed every moment. If I ever had a moment where I felt like I was going to die, that would have been it. I would be trying to write out my homework in one hand and throwing up in a bucket in the other. That was basically my life for two weeks. While I was being isolated in my room, I felt like I was separated from the world and I wasn't even a part of this earth anymore. I would try over and over again to keep a positive attitude and I always tried remember in the back of my mind that God had a plan for me.

September 2nd, was the day of my surgery. I would be lying if I said I wasn't nervous. The biggest fear I had going into surgery was not waking up from it. I was literally putting my life into the doctor's hands. I guess the nurses sensed I was a little shaky about all of it; so, as I was getting my pre-op done and, then, finally getting rolled into the operating room, they stuck me with the I.V. in my arm. I have never done drugs in all my life; but I can say on that day I was feeling pretty dang good. I was trying to have conversations with everyone like they were my friends or something. And, I could of swore that I heard two of the male nurses talking about fantasy football while they were putting on their latex gloves. Soon enough the nurses told me to count to one hundred and I only made it to three. At that point it was all in God's hands.

CHAPTER 3

Trophies

When people say that you'll have the best sleep in your life during surgery, they're completely right. The nurses were trying to wake me up and all I wanted to do was sleep. Everytime I woke up for a quick second there was someone different in the recovery room- whether it was another family member, friend, and I think even a pastor. I still to this day have no clue who he was. I remember one of the nurses giving me the remote to my bed, the TV, and the lights in the room. That was a big mistake on my nurse's part because the pain medicine was still flowing through my body. I pressed every button on the remote and every light in the room started to flicker, like some kind of light show. Everyone around me was laughing pretty hard at my behavior; but, I was so drugged up on pain meds I didn't realize what I was doing. I felt very weak at times and it was hard to keep my eyes open long enough to have a conversation with somebody. I had I.V.'s stuck all over my body and even a needle that was as long as a toothpick pierced into the side of my neck. That needs was mainly to drain out any excess fluid in my neck. I looked like a lab experiment and that's what I felt like too. I was stuck in the hospital for a week and a half and all I did from morning till night was lie in the bed, eat, and take a shower. You never realize how much you take for granted until everything you took for granted is taken away from you. A simple shower that usually took five minutes now took about twenty minutes. Some people may laugh when I say this, but it was so tough my dad had to help me bathe myself. Days before I could go home, the nurses wanted me to walk around in the hallway to start gaining strength back in my legs. My legs felt numb almost like I didn't have any to stand on. This was like the base of my life; the "rock" I stood on had changed directions and now stood on me. It was like teaching a baby how to walk for the first time. The hospital had railings on the walls that I held on to so tightly that my veins in my hands were popping out. While I was walking I had a nurse in front of me, to the side of me, and my dad was behind me. It was kinda funny because it felt like I had some bodyguards around me.

After being in the hospital for almost two weeks I was finally released to go home and it felt great to finally leave. All the nurses and staff were very nice but I was glad to go home and eat something a little better than hospital food. Many nights at home I would have to sleep on the couch sitting upright and try to be as still as possible. Don't get me wrong I enjoyed my parents getting me things when I asked; but then again I felt bad because I know they were getting tired of catering to me all the time. I tried to do as much as I can on my own and even when I knew I couldn't do something I would still try anyways. Everything I did hurt my neck, even laughing hurt at times. I had felt a sense of helplessness and was becoming more and more frustrated as the time went on, there were nights when my parents went to bed and I would sit in the living room in complete darkness simply talking to God. One of the two people who would understand my anger besides my uncle who was fighting cancer alongside with me. I would question God and his power. "Why me, why are you putting me through this pain and frustration?" It would bring me to tears thinking about the road that lay ahead for me and my uncle.

It was 2013 and the Boston Red Sox were in the World Series. that was me and my uncle's favorite baseball team. Being able to watch the game and then talk about it with my uncle, kept my mind off of all the bad things that were happening around me- and it gave me something to do besides worry. My uncle and I watched every game together except the last game of the World Series; because he had to go back to a hospital in Baltimore, Maryland for chemotherapy treatments. Although chemo didn't stop him from watching the game and talking about it with me. He watched it from his hospital room and I watched the game from my bedroom and we texted each other throughout the whole game. To this day I still have the text messages we texted each other throughout the game. The Red Sox games were a way for my uncle and me to forget about the chemo, the radiation, and the cancer. Baseball gave us something to enjoy together. After the Red Sox won the World Series, we didn't stop texting each other until 4 a.m. in the morning because we were so excited our team had actually won the whole thing!

My uncle was always there when I needed to talk to him. It didn't matter what time of the day it was, he would always talk to me and I really needed him when I started to go back to school again. My doctor had told me I wasn't allowed to carry anything over ten pounds; so, that meant someone had to carry my book bag for me. One of my teachers had a girl who was a cheerleader carry my bags and she had her own bags to carry as well. I felt really bad having her carry my stuff for me because my book bag weighed a ton and I knew it wasn't an easy task for her to do. So I asked my assistant principal if I could have a specific person carry my bags around full-time until I was able to again. And with that said, the next day I was called back to the office to see who was going to carry my stuff. My mind was going into circles as I was thinking who could it be and I was very happy when I found out who it was. It was one of my buddies on the football team named Blake and this dude was built. He was a senior and played tight end and was very tall." I asked him "Are you sure you want to do this?" and he replied back with "Absolutely, I'll carry you in one arm and your stuff in the other." We built a good friendship with each other and we would always pick with each other, since he was a giant. I would always call him tiny which he obviously wasn't but I liked picking with him. With him carrying my bags in school I would always get weird looks from other people but I would just try to ignore them because it was embarrassing for me as it was and I didn't want any attention put on me. Some days I didn't want to go to school and instead just lie in bed and talk with my uncle. When I talked to him I felt happy again. It felt like all the weight was off my shoulders for those couple of hours. School for me didn't feel like a learning experience anymore, more like a judging zone. I lost a lot of friends, one's I thought that would stick by my side and I would grow old with someday. Everyone at school started to put a label on me as "the boy who has cancer" because heaven forbid if you were ever caught talking with me you might lose popularity, but all I was looking for was someone just to listen to me, listen to my many struggles and frustrating obstacles. One night as I was sitting in my bedroom I was thinking in my mind "should I just be homeschooled?" I prayed about it long and hard and asked God to lead me into the right direction and to simply show me guidance. It felt like it was God-sent because not even a minute after I prayed, my phone buzzed and it was my uncle. He asked how my day went at school and I told him upfront that it was miserable and everybody seemed to think I was contagious or something. Nowadays, I was going to school not focused on learning but only focused on what people were saying behind my back. There were many times where I was told that I was faking everything and I was pathetic for wanting attention and I was a disappointment to my parents. This issue did not stop once I got home either, I would get text messages from random numbers texting me some very vulgar comments that were hard to even repeat out loud. I never told anyone this before and only my uncle knew this at the time. I explained to him how I wanted to end it all and just commit suicide, I had enough pills to own a pharmacy with all of my prescription meds I owned. I also thought about just not taking my synthroid pill which keeps me alive as well, it was the first time I actually thought about death and it was a scary time for me. I went on for weeks trying to decide if this is what I actually wanted to do, if ending it would make everything better and taking me out of the picture completely was the best scenario at the time. He was the only person who knew this brokenness about me and I can honestly say my uncle saved me. He told me something that day I will never forget, he said "Bailey, that scar you have on your neck don't be ashamed of it but just embrace it and show it off, that scar is a trophy and you earned it Beatle. Not many people have a trophy like yours; so instead of worrying on how it looks or what other people think about it, just be proud of it. Don't ask God why he gave you a scar on your neck just thank him that he did." He always knew what to say at the right time and it made me think about life in a new perspective where I shouldn't questioned God's work but just accept anything he throws into my life and to embrace the good and the bad.

CHAPTER 4

Turning Point

For a long time my life felt like it was on hold. I couldn't be the teenager I wanted to be and do the things I wanted to do like hanging out with friends and playing football, the sport I loved. But, that had all changed a few months later when my doctor called the house phone saying he wanted me to come into his doctor's office, as soon as possible. My parents and I had no clue what it was for, but we didn't waste any time in making an appointment to see him- and this time my dad made sure he was with us. As I sat in the back seat of the car, I just reflected on what all has happened to me this past year.

I remembered sitting in bed countless nights feeling horrible due to migraine headaches and throwing up. I remembered crying and pleading to God asking him to make the pain go away. I realized who my true friends were and who the fake friends were. I remembered thinking about being home schooled. And, I even remembered the nights I would let it all out and complain to my uncle about all my frustrations until I crashed and fell asleep. A lot had happened that year and this was the first time I actually reflected on all of it. There was no telling what the doctor was going to say, but I was ready for whatever he had to tell me. Of course, we showed up early because we were getting anxious and we're hoping he could see us sooner. I signed in and sat in the waiting room trying to waste some time by flipping through a Sports Illustrated magazine. While I was skimming through it I saw an article on Eric Berry, a famous NFL football player who was diagnosed with Hodgkin's Lymphoma. He explained his day to day life of having cancer and he talked about similar struggles that

I also had while battling cancer. He went on to explain how things in life aren't going to be handed to you and it's going to be difficult; but, the real questioned he asked was "Are you going let your problems crush you? Or are you going to harness your problems and take them under your wing?" Throughout this journey of mine I kept that question in my head, "Am I going be defeated by cancer or am I going to take the bull by the horns and kick cancer's tail?"

Finally, one of the nurses came out the door calling for me; I immediately jumped out of my seat and I went speed walking all the way to the door. Right as I turned the corner, I was checked for my height and weight and eventually made it to one of the examining rooms. I remember constantly asking my parents a bunch of questions about what they thought was going on and, of course, they knew as much as me, which was little to none at this point. Of course the doctor didn't come into the room immediately; so, my inner child kicked in and I started to play with the latex gloves and blow them up to the point when they're about to pop. I heard a slight knock on the door and I quickly tried to get rid of the glove by putting it in the trash can before the doctor caught me. I could tell a change in tone in his voice, a much happier tone than the last visit; he shook my hand and sat down and asked me how I was doing and I told him I was good, but a little anxious.

He said "Well, the reason why I called y'all in here today is because I have some pretty great news."

Me and my parents looked at each other thinking the same thing, was it finally over? Was I cancer free? The doctor went on to explain that after looking at my most recent scans and blood work he came to a conclusion that the cancer was nowhere to be found and that I was cancer free! And yes, you can probably guess what happened after that, I literally sprung out of my chair and hugged my parents for a good five minutes. All of us were in tears, including my doctor, but they were tears of joy and complete excitement. It had also felt like I was dreaming; because I thought I'd never hear those words come out of my doctor's mouth. Finally, I felt like in my life I was in control again, and it felt exhilarating!

CHAPTER 5

#10

Everything seemed to be back to normal again. I was going back to school more often and raising my grades back up in the process. One morning, as my mom was driving me to school, she seemed a little disturbed; so I asked her, "what was the matter?" She replied "I didn't want to tell you because I'm sure it's just a false alarm, but uncle Dan is in the hospital right now and said he wasn't doing too good as of right now." I was a little worried after she said that, but while I was in the car with my mom and didn't really say anything after her last comment. But, I just sat there staring out the window, all the way until we got to school. The day went by a little uneasily as I went to class to class, not focusing on the assignments that were given to me, but in a daze thinking about what my mom said that morning and wondering how my uncle was doing and how he was feeling. As I walked into my last class, I sat down and got a couple of things out of my book bag that I needed. It wasn't even fifteen minutes into class and the intercom came on and asked for me to get my stuff together to leave. It was a rare occasion for me to leave school early; so, I knew that there had to be a reason why I was leaving. When I heard the front office calling for me to leave the first thing that popped in my head was my uncle; and I quickly got a sick feeling in my stomach. I walked out of the hallway, and once I saw that no teachers or administration walking around outside, I bolted to the car lot to search for my mom's car; and sure enough it was sitting there with a very upset mom in the driver's seat. I wanted to ask her a thousand questions, but seeing her sobbing I didn't know what to say or ask; so, I sat there in the passenger's seat incomplete silence. Finally, she spoke to me and said "We're going to the house real quick to meet your dad and to take some spare clothes with us. We're going to Charlotte to see Uncle Dan, because the doctors don't know how much more time he has to live." My uncle was at a hospital in the heart of Charlotte, because he lived around that area. When we got home, I immediately went to my room and started to pack some clothes to last me about a week. This whole time I was doing pretty well with holding my tears back, but my dad came into my room and asked "Are you okay with everything?" And that's when the floodgates to my eyes had finally opened and I started to cry hugging my dad, drenching his shirt in tears. The last time I cried like that was when I heard I was diagnosed with cancer. Once we all got our things packed into the car, we started to head to Charlotte. The car ride there was full of sadness and three very depressed people. I put my headphones on and tried to calm down a little by taking a little nap before we arrived at the hospital. Once we got there we had to sign in saying that we were family and I was told to put on a mask that I had to wear while we were in the room seeing him. My parents and I walked in the room to see of course my uncle but also my family, we all sat around him while he was cracking jokes to all of us like there was nothing wrong with him. He always knew how to lighten the mood and find even an ounce of positivity, taking our minds off of all the bad things that were happening at that moment. It was so sad to see my best friend suffering and not being able to do anything about it. He would hallucinate a lot as he would try to swat imaginary flies from his face. I sat in the corner of the room on a stepping stool with my face buried in my arms and knees. I couldn't stop crying because all I could think about was my uncle suffering and at that moment my dad saw me and asked if I wanted to take a walk. Well, I didn't make it two feet out of the door until I sat back down and started to cry some more. My dad wrapped his arms around me with a blanket of comfort trying to cheer me up in every way possible. The nurses at a nearby desk saw the two of us and kindly asked if we wanted to go into a room. We both agreed and the nurse and my dad both walked me to the room so I could calm down a little and regroup myself. About thirty minutes after sitting in that room, my uncle's wife knocked quietly on the door and asked how I was doing. I told her that I was doing better and then she went on to mention that my uncle would like to see me.

Staggering back into his room, I made myself to his bedside and quickly hugged him. The first thing he whispered in my ear was that he was sorry for not being there to watch the final game of the World Series with me. After all that he was going through at that moment he apologized to me and it broke my heart to hear that from him. I whispered in his ear and said that I loved him so much and thanked him for being my best friend through all the ups and downs and never leaving my side. The very last thing he said to me was "keep the number ten alive Beatle." The number ten was his favorite number and his softball number as well, that number runs in our family and to us it means more than just a number. When my uncle told me that I promised him I would keep the number ten alive for him by wearing it as my football number next season. That night some of our family spent the night at the hospital in the waiting room down the hall and if you ever have seen packed sardines before, that's what we looked like that night as we tried to sleep. One of my cousins, named Ziggy, spent the night as well at the hospital and he's a super tall guy. I would take a guess and say he's at least 6'4" and he managed to put some chairs in a row and squirmed his way underneath all the armrest, so he could sleep on the set of chairs. It was a funny sight to see one of the tallest guys in the room has the smallest space. Right outside the window, was the landing spot for emergency helicopters; so, throughout the night when I couldn't sleep, I watched the helicopters fly in and out all night. As the sunrise was beginning to rise I was the only one awake as everyone else was still asleep. I walked around the hallways reflecting on everything that has happened so far and it's all been one big nightmare that I couldn't wake up from. I came back to the waiting room where everyone was still asleep and laid back in my chair and began to pray once more, praying for a miracle that somehow my uncle will beat this cancer and will be well again and that this nightmare of a life will soon cease. 9 o'clock rolled around and everyone was started to wake up. My mom and dad left the hospital to go pick up breakfast for everyone at a McDonald's down the street. As we were eating, everyone's mood seemed to lighten up and we were all talking about various things like sports, weather, and how good McDonald's hash browns were. As the hours in the day past we left the hospital and stayed at my cousin's house, which was near Charlotte. The doctor told all of us that my uncle was coming home and was going to be taken off of life support. So, after we dropped off our entire luggage at my cousin's house, we all drove over to my uncle's house to go see him. He was sitting in a bed that looked like a hospital bed in his living room and all he had hooked up to him was an oxygen tank. It was hard for him to keep his eyes open and he couldn't speak a lot anymore-seeing someone you love being slowing taken away from you is the worst feeling in the world. I couldn't imagine what he was feeling at that moment, but if I could have traded positions with him I would have done it in a heartbeat. My mom sat beside him holding his hands while she was crying and she didn't leave his side the whole night while we were there. Some more family members came as well but looking around the room, everyone was a little uneasy. Mom and I both sitting on the armrest of the couch close to my uncle, others were talking about other things to lighten the mood and others were in separate parts of the house having their alone time to basically process of what was to come. It was 10 p.m. now and my cousins and I were leaving, but my mom and my uncle's daughter, Denise spent the night at his house to be with him. Once we arrived at my cousin's house we didn't stay up any longer and went to bed. My dad and I slept on two beds that were beside each other. Before we went to bed, we starting talking to each other about all the good times we had with him. Like the times we went hunting with him and he would always try to make me laugh in the tree stand, and the time we went to the beach and my mom fed him grapes like he was a king or some sort. The little things like that brought a big smile to my face because I still laugh at those moments today. It was 12 in morning and my dad's phone buzzed, it was my mom and she texted us saying "Uncle Dan just passed away." January 31st, 2015 was the day he passed away. The fact that he wasn't with us anymore didn't really sink in that night. Early that next morning we got up and drove back over to my uncle's house. When we got there the bed where my uncle was lying at was no longer there, it was just an empty space. My mom was sitting with my uncle's daughter at the kitchen table still in tears; so we came over to sit with them and comfort them. Soon after we arrived, so did their pastor and his wife with breakfast. As we sat down and ate we discussed his funeral and how it would all be planned out. Then a question was asked towards me and I was asked if I wanted to say a few words at his funeral in front of everybody. If you know me personally, I don't like public speaking but this was something different, for everything he had done for me the least I could do was speak for him. After thinking about it I agreed to do it. I thought long and hard about what I should say and I couldn't figure out the right thing to say about him, because I wanted it to be perfect. The next week rolled around and it was time for his funeral. We had gotten at the church really early to rehearse a little and to make sure everything was set up properly. We had his bike that he named Wally parked in the church, along with posters of pictures of him and our family with captured memories with him. Before the funeral started Denise, who was my uncle's daughter and my cousin's mom wanted me and my cousins to come out into the hallway. She pulled a box for each of us and told us to open it, it was a dog tag necklace that had the number ten engraved on one side and on the other was a saying that was in Italian. It said "Il mio dio e piu di abbastanza" which meant "my God is more than enough." My uncle lived by that saying as he went through his own battle with cancer. That necklace means everything me and I still wear it to this day. As the funeral started they began talking about my uncle and then soon enough the band started to play a couple of songs and a slideshow that followed. Soon enough it was my time to speak and as I was thinking about what I should say about my uncle, I went a different route and wrote something that everyone could relate to. The title of it was "What Cancer Cannot Do", It said "cancer cannot cripple love, it cannot shatter hope, it cannot corrode faith, and it cannot destroy peace, it cannot kill friendships, it cannot suppress memories, and it cannot silence courage, it cannot invade the soul, cancer cannot steal eternal life, and it cannot conquer the spirit."

CHAPTER 6

Joshua 1:9

After losing my uncle, I felt like a piece of my heart was missing. Having someone around for such a long time and now in a blink of an eye he was gone. It took me a long time to get used to the fact. At times it had felt like a dream, but in this case I wasn't going to wake up anytime soon. Summer was quickly ending and my junior year was about to begin. The last time I was in school my uncle was still alive; so, starting the new school year was definitely tough for me. I can still remember my first day of my junior year because it wasn't just an ordinary day; it was something special that eventually changed my life. Of course, on the first day of school you're a little nervous about who's in your class, who will be at your lunch, and who your teachers would be. I had math for my first block class and as I walked in I was greeted by my teacher at the door as he said good morning and shook my hand, so far I was getting good vibes from my first teacher and felt like I was going to enjoy this class. He told me to look for my name on one of the desks and once I finally found where it was I noticed it was close to the teacher's desk and I was seated towards the front door. What I also noticed was that a very pretty girl was sitting behind me. The first thing that came to my mind was that there was no way in the world that she was single. I remember when I saw her, I wasn't sure if she was giving me a dirty look or if she was just mad that it was the first day of school, because she did not seem very happy. My goal that semester was not to act weird around her and to not say anything stupid. Every morning in class I would try to think about things to say to her and every time I had the opportunity, I would get all choked up and I could never build up the courage to talk to her. Eventually, our teacher told the class we had to get into small groups to work on assignments in class, and I was paired with her. I was definitely nervous at first because she was way smarter than I was and I didn't want to say anything stupid to make her not like me; but; it was the total opposite. We clicked almost instantly and we would talk to each other for the whole class period, while also getting really good at playing paper football in the meantime. I found out her name was Skylar and we both had things in common, for instance we both played sports and we didn't like school, which I think every student can relate to that last part. As the days went on in school I started have feelings for her and I felt like she was that missing piece in my heart that I was missing for a long time. At that point in the school year it was football season and one of our big games was coming up. So, that Friday of the big game I asked Skylar if she could come and at first she didn't know if she was going or not but after begging her to go she said she'll be there and for the rest of the day I was the happiest kid at school. During pregame, as the team was warming up on the field, I would constantly look up in the stands to see if she was sitting in the bleachers-but I didn't see her. Everytime that I came off of the field I would glance up at the stands, but I didn't see her. At that point, I was wondering if she even showed up to the game and I was getting a little upset. After the game was over, the team headed towards the end zone; and following that my head coach talked to us reflecting on the game we just played. After we broke up and walked to the fences to meet our family, a girl with a pink jacket walked through the crowd towards me; it was Skylar. I was shocked, but at the same time so happy to see her at the game supporting me! I quickly hugged her and asked her where she was all this time during the game. She said "Yeah, I saw you looking up in the stands, but you never looked right in front of you." She literally sat in the front row and I never saw her. We continued to talk and laugh about the situation and one of her friends walked by us and then whispered to Skylar asking if we were dating then we both looked at each other and smiled and she said "I don't know" which we weren't at the time but we both didn't want to say no at the same time. It made the moment kinda awkward and I got a little red in the face when her friend asked the question. But, it was good to know from her comment that she did have feelings for me too and for her to show up to the game to support me meant the world to me and it showed that she really did care about me. We continued to talk more and more every day in math class learning more and more about each other than the actual assignment that was given to us and eventually we started dating each other at the end of my junior year.

CHAPTER 7

Isaiah 40:29-31

With junior year quickly ended and my senior year was approaching even more quickly. My senior year began with summer football workouts. Between the dead heat of the summer and doing drills and lifting I could honestly say that I was counting down the hours to go home. Although I knew everything that we have done during the summer would pay-off on Fridays and I had to keep that mindset working all the way up to the first football game. I missed some the summer practices because I was involved in something else during the summer. I went to a summer program called Elon Academy where I spent all four summers of high school learning and having the college experience. We would actually have college classes and live in the dorm rooms to basically get a feel of what college is actually like. So, when I came back to training camp I had to earn my starting spot all over again. When I came back there was one more scrimmage before the season actually started. I knew that I had to play harder than I ever had before because I knew this could make or break my opportunity to be a starter for the upcoming season. During the first scrimmage, I didn't get much playing time because my position coach put in a teammate who was at training camp all summer. When I came back I knew I worked to my greatest ability, and I even stayed after practice to work on different drills. When I was benched for the first game, a world of emotions came over me. Then I had finally got my chance to play, I wanted to prove to the coaches that I could play well enough to be a starter. During a scrimmage my position coach told me I was starting the next series, but in my mind I told myself that would not be coming out of the game after

28

that. I would not give my coaches reason to take me out. I was already angry that I sat out of the last game. On the third play, I rushed off the edge, hawked down the quarterback, and made the sack in the backfield. During the next series I was back on the field. I intercepted the ball and ran it back for a touchdown. I never came out of that game, just like I told myself I wouldn't. When training camp had finally ended, we began working towards our first game of the season. Every practice was not only a day to get better, but it was also an opportunity to keep a starting job I worked so hard for. I knew that being the first to practice and the last to leave was what it was going to take to stay on top of my game and earn that starting job.

As the season started to come into play, I was earning my spot to play each and every week. My favorite game of my senior season was homecoming. We were announced as the game of the week for that game; and the stands were so full that people were forced to sit on the hills. I remember going to our pre-game meal where we all sit down as a team and eat together, we would always hear devotion for the game and at the very end when we would be close to leaving our head coach would announce our two honorary captains for the game. Every Friday, coach picked two people who he thought performed at their best throughout the week. Usually before coach announced whom the captains were going to be me and my teammates who sat with me guessed to see who was going to captains. One of the captains he picked was my friend Michael who was sitting across from me at the table; and coach talked about his strong work ethic. And then, coach started to talk about the next captain. Coach started to describe this man not necessarily as the strongest or the biggest person on the field, but he said this guy is definitely the strongest off the field. The way he was describing this person, it sounded like it could be me; but I didn't want to give up my hopes, so I kept the excitement bottled up inside me. Coach then began talking about the touchy subject of cancer; and once he mentioned that word, my heart sank because I knew for sure now he was talking about me. He went on to say that "The good people in life are the ones who get beat down the most but for Bailey he learned to adapt to his challenges and never gave up when things got rough." It meant a lot to me that he said that to the whole team; it made me realize that people did notice my hard work ethic and drive on and off the field.

At this team meal, things were a little different and it shocked all of us about what happened. As we were finishing up dinner, coach said that our parents wrote each of us a little something. Everyone was called up to get an envelope that had our names on it. There was one moment that I'll never forget that day. Austin, my one of many best friends, said that "I doubt I'll get anything." Austin went on to say that he didn't think his dad would take the time to write him a letter. As soon as Austin said that, coach called his name and he had the most confused look on his face. He came back, sat down next to me, and before he even opened it, he started crying. All he had seen on the letter was his dad's name written across the envelope. His dad wrote him the letter that he thought he would never receive. I got one letter from my dad and one letter from my mom. Both letters had the same idea, same message, and same love. My parents wrote about what I had been through battling cancer, experiencing my first death, and also telling me they loved me very much. At the end of the letter, after reading all the sad and emotional stuff, my dad wrote at the bottom of the letter "P.S. make sure you play hard tonight and hit them first." Yeah that sounds like my dad, always had to coach me up before every game, I thought.

When we got back to the school to get ready for the game, there were cars already pulling in the parking lot. After getting taped up, I went into another room and kneeled down and prayed by myself. I thanked God for the opportunities thrown my way, to be captain, to being to play the sport I love, and even I thanked him for me having cancer, because without it I would have never of realized how strong I really could be. Opportunities like that night only come once in a lifetime and I was very blessed to be able to strap on the pads that night and play in front of that crowd. After our position meetings, I sat back at my locker and took out a sharpie out of my bag. On my wrist tape I put a cancer symbol and my uncle's favorite number. I finally put my shoulder pads on and then put my eye black; I would put it on every game always the same way, never different-one thick streak under both eyes and used three fingers to run it down my face. It was getting close to game time and I could hear the roar of the crowd and the loud thumping of the marching band all the way in the locker room. As chills ran through my spine, I couldn't think of a better situation to be in at that point- it was all so perfect. When we walked down to the practice field to warm up, multiple cars for the parade were already lined up. As the time came to actually go down to the game field, we walked down a different path to get down to the field. As one of the captains we had to be in the front of the team as we walked down to the field. As fans were looking for us at our normal entrance we shocked our home crowd and went up through the bleachers were our fan base sat and the crowd went insane. People were high fiving us as we walked by them and hitting our shoulder pads and helmets getting us hyped up. While walking through the bleachers with our fan base roaring in our ears, it gave me chills and made my energy level go through the roof. The only bad thing that happened that night was that we lost, but so much more happened that night that was so special: starting with our pre-game meal, being captain, receiving a letter from my parents, walking out through our fans for homecoming for the very last time.

It was starting to get later into the season and our games were dwindling down pretty fast. After homecoming our schedule was pretty laid back and we also had a week off because of our bye week. Even though the little break we had was nice we had to get back to work and focus on a big game that was coming our way. The big game I'm talking about is Dudley high school and when I say their players were big I mean they were grown men. Most people would never think twice about playing them in football and throughout that week, mysteriously players were all of the sudden getting injured. Dudley has a reputation for being state champions and they definitely prove why they are champions when they play. After our walk through practice on Thursday coach sat us down and told us that Dudley scheduled us for their homecoming. Sure it isn't the best news in the world but they always seem to have us play them for homecoming every year. Dudley's homecoming is like no other, it honestly feels like a college football game, there would be grilling tints, inflatable bouncy houses, and they would even have A&T's band play alongside with their band. It would make you so pumped up to play with all the action going on around you that you would start to forget that it's not even your homecoming. Warming up on the field I think was the hardest task to do out of everything involving our routine stretching. While stretching we were sitting on the field next to all the food stands with all the amazing smells coming from the food trucks. My stomach was starting to growl and as a team we just ate an hour before that. The sights and sounds of a game like that is something you have to experience firsthand because with all the extra stuff going on that builds up to kick off its honestly something special. Not only were the sights and sounds of the game so overwhelming, something else that night changed my life forever.

CHAPTER 8

Game Changer

Three minutes were left on the scoreboard that counted down until game time and the team was waiting to bust through our banner. To the far side of the field were our opponents who were jumping up and down, the band playing right behind them as their dancers made a tunnel for them. Once we heard the announcer say "And here are your Southern Alamance Patriots" we sprinted through the banner towards the sideline to meet our fan base in the stands. 12:00, and were kicking it to Dudley and they run it back to our 40 yard line. It was our first time on defense and I was doing pretty well, I made some tackles and I even jammed the receivers on the line. I was starting to get into the flow of things after my nerves started to settle down. Dudley drove the ball down the field within seconds and they punched the ball in for six points at the goal line from a play action play that had us all fooled. 10:33 was on the clock as they kicked it off to us and I was on the second row on the receiving team. Their kicker literally kicked the ball passed the end zone but before we realized that the ball was out of bounce we were already looking for someone to block. As I went down the field I targeted one person and I went to go block him, at the same time he wanted to knock me flat on my back. In all four years of playing high school football I had never been hit by someone so hard in my life. We collided into each other and both stood each other up but during that same moment I went to plant my leg back into the ground, my leg just gave out on me. When I went to plant my foot into the ground, my knee felt like it shifted and came back in its regular position. I laid on the ground for a couple of minutes to reassure myself that I wasn't dead but once I decided to get up my leg wouldn't move and that's when I knew I was in some serious trouble.

After that I stayed on the ground starting to feel the pain that was coming to my knee. I had no clue what my leg looked like, if I broke it or something was dislocated but what I knew for sure is that my leg was not fine. The trainer rushed over to check my leg and then my coach came over to check on me as well, our trainer coach G told me that I need to go on the training table to be looked at more carefully. Well at this point I can't walk at all on my leg but somehow I had to get to the training table, before I even thought about getting up two of my teammates picked me up like a small dog and carried me to the training table. Once I was seated on the training table coach G examined my knee and was shaking his head the whole time. At the time, all he told me was that I tore a ligament in my knee but he wasn't sure which ligament it was so he recommended I take a trip to the hospital that night to get an MRI done. I sat there for a moment and come to realize that my high school football career is over; I would never play another down of football in my high school career. It wasn't even five minutes into the game and I was already hurt. Coach G called down my dad from the stands and told him to come down so he could tell him what all is going on, I started to cry because football was over for me and most importantly I felt like I disappointed my dad. I threw a towel over my head and continued to cry for the rest of the time I was there. As I was waiting to be transported to a vehicle to go to the hospital one of my other coaches walked up to me with something in his hand...it was my mouthpiece. Let me also mention this, the dude that hit me was committed to Auburn and he definitely proved to me why he was going to play ball there.

By the time we left from the game until we made to the hospital my knee was as big as a softball ball. By this time it was around 2 o'clock as we were waiting in the waiting room, as I sat in the wheelchair, the pain in my knee wasn't the issue it was the pain that was going inside me knowing that high school football was forever over. As I got called back the nurses had me x rayed to see if any bones were broken and sure enough everything came back negative which meant that it was most likely a ligament tear in my knee. My parents and I asked the doctor so many questions of many possibilities it could be and the doctor explained how it's definitely a ligament tear but wasn't sure which ligament yet, he said "if anything you rather have MCL tear than an ACL tear because the recovery time for an ACL is much longer." So he scheduled an appointment to get an MRI done the following weeks so we can figure out what to do about this whole process. I was hoping and praying that it wasn't an ACL tear because in that case I would need surgery and I'm not a big fan of that. Weeks later we got the results back from the doctor and again he wanted us to make a visit to his office to explain everything personally. Once we got there and were put into one of their examining rooms the doctor quickly came in after and said "Sadly it's an ACL tear and you're done for the rest of the season." I kinda figured that was the case because weeks after the injury occurred I still felt extreme sharp pain and I couldn't walk on it at all. One of my greatest fears arose again as I would have to face another surgery and be put under once again. Even having my first surgery when I had cancer I'm still afraid to this day to not waking up from surgery. None of this didn't seem real at all until I actually schedule a surgery date and also when I couldn't practice with the team anymore. Again it felt like my life was spiraling out of control and my senior year was on the same path.

It was December and it was time for my surgery. 7:00 in the morning was the time I was supposed to be there and it was an hour after we got there until they actually called me back for surgery. At first I was doing pretty good and not getting worried and as time went on I started to get more and more nervous. An old coach of mine, coach Bishop, my parents, and someone very special to me, my girlfriend, was there. Skylar talked with me the whole time to try to get my mind off of it and to calm my nerves down a little bit. She brings a book bag with her and I was thinking that she was going to do some school work while she was there but little did I know it was far from homework. She whipped out a bunch of coloring books and to be funny she also took out a barf bag and said "you might need this." You would have thought she brought her whole house with her. After the wait was over and I finally got called back the nurses there told me to get undressed and put on a gown with some weird looking socks. I guess the nurses sensed I was a little nervous because they stuck an I.V. in my arm and gave me some medicine to chill out and calm down. I could sense the medicine was working because I wanted to have a conversation with everybody in the hospital. I got wheeled into the operating room and they had me lie down on the operating table and one of the nurse said "We're gonna have you take off your underwear as well." At the time I didn't know if that was the medicine talking or I actually heard her correctly. Soon they put an oxygen mask over my face. "Count to ten" the nurse said, and by that time I reached to three and I was out once again.

When waking up I was in a daze like you wouldn't believe, along with my girlfriend I also had my friend there as well, he's basically my brother and my mom asked if I knew who was there and I said "of course I do SpongeBob and Patrick!" They got a kick out of that, along with me being freaked out by the blood pressure cuff around my arm. Once I returned home that day and started to feel less loopy I started to feel the pain more and more. I unwrapped my bandages from my leg and saw the large scar going down the front of my knee, two little scars on the side of my knee. It was times like this where I thought it was impossible for me to come back from this injury and play sports again. At times when I would have to use the bathroom I would need assistance or even get into or out of bed. I had to sit on the edge of my bed while either my mom or dad had to lift up my leg so I could lie down. Even the slightest move would make me go into tears because of the pain that shot down my leg. When I went to school I would bring extra clothes because using crutches would make me sweat so badly and to add on to it people would stare everyday I used crutches. I honestly felt miserable and I wanted to rewind into the past to the Dudley game to where I never got hurt. I always thought to myself if I could have done something differently to prevent me from getting injured and how my life would have been different without worrying about tearing my ACL. Knowing the long journey ahead of me, I took the time to think about football and what the future holds for me. After thinking and praying long and hard about my decision, I decided I was not going to play football ever again. I had offers to play football in college and I stood firm on my decision. I was at a point in my life when I didn't understand what God wanted me to do and I was very confused about the path he was leading me towards. I felt like I needed to take a break from football and focus on myself. Whether that may be another sport or letting that career path seize. With tearing my ACL I believed it was a sign from God and I took that as a hint to lean towards another direction in my life, a direction I had not yet discovered.

CHAPTER 9

On the Rise

My life building up to now would consist of physical therapy and a whole lot of grit. If I wanted to play again I had to be so determined and motivated than I've ever been before. My process of recovery was going to take the span of a year before I am back at one hundred percent. During my first PT appointment I was still on crutches and the first thing my trainer made me do was to go on the stationary bike and tried to peddle. I was at the point where I couldn't make a full rotation on the bike and I couldn't even do heel raises without any assistance and by the end of each session my leg would just feel like a dead weight that I was dragging around. I can't express to you how physical therapy sucked, it was the most smallest exercises you could think of but they were so hard for me to do. One of the exercises I had to put a weighted ankle bracelet around my good leg at first. I did fifteen reps or so with no problem at, although; getting to my bad leg it was a struggles to lift it up. My trainer had to assist me at times to make sure I got every rep. Don't get me wrong, some days were actually pretty fun not because of the exercise but the elderly women who would gossip with me about their husbands and give me relationship advice. If you would have told me years ago that I would be getting relationship advice from some elderly women on an exercise table I would have laughed and called you crazy.

Well before I even had PT, my brother and I went Christmas shopping and of course he had to drive and that was the last time I drove with him while I was on crutches. The reason is that before we went shopping we decided to catch a movie, but instead of driving close to the door and being kind and showing sympathy, he decides to park in the very back of the parking lot, so I asked what we were doing so far away and he said "you can walk or crutch like your doc said to." I still didn't see why we had to park so far away but all he could say was that it was good for me. Throughout my long process of excesses and icing my knee like crazy the pain and swelling seemed to go down and I actually felt like I could walk on it more. Every day I would make little goals for myself to walk certain distances, for example I would work all week to walk from my kitchen table to the living room couch. When I reached my goal and I would try to do longer distances to make it harder and more challenging on myself. I'm the kind of person who likes to prove the impossible and prove to doubters that I can do something even though other people said I couldn't. That's why when the doctor said I could put as much weight on my leg as I want it was just depending on how much pain tolerance I had. Later on the following week I went back to see my surgeon to cut the stitches out of my leg and that was a very happy moment in my life because once I got the stitches out I felt like I could start bending my leg and I could walk better. Once I got my stitches out of my knee, my physical therapist made me do leg curls and leg extensions with a five pound ankle weight. Those five pounds felt like twenty pounds on my leg, it was the simplest of workouts but with my leg still in rehab, it was a much more challenging task to overcome. Throughout my process of physical therapy and doctor visits my leg has gotten progressively better and I feel like I've overcome another obstacle in my life, during the past four years a lot has happened to me that have changed my life forever.

CHAPTER 10

Ecclesiastes 3:1

As the summer of my senior year was finally here, I took this time to spend it with my friends and family the most. I remember a week after my graduation me and a couple of my friends all went to Myrtle Beach for senior week. I have to say it was a long week but there was never a dull moment, starting off the week by going to out to eat at Broadway at the Beach. As we ate we tried to plan out the week of what we all wanted to do, which we plenty of time to figure it all out. We all finished our first night by walking around and checking out all the stores and watching a pretty awesome firework show. As the week progressed we spent plenty of days hanging out on the beach, playing football and swimming in the ocean. A couple nights before we had to go back home, I was sitting at the pool with my friend Austin. We knew once we got back home we would have to start thinking about college what we wanted to do career wise.

Before senior week me and Austin had our signing day when we declared where we were going to go and play lacrosse and football. Me and Austin had offers to play at a few schools, but we felt like Averett and Wingate University was the best fit for us at the time. So fast forwarding to when we were hanging out by the pool, we reflected on our senior year and how much we have changed throughout high school until now. We considered going to the same school so we could room together but we could never find the right school for both of us to be happy at. Trust me I begged him to come to Averett with me because I knew he had an offer to play football there but his heart was set on Wingate and I knew that he had to do what was best for his career. He had to go to college early because he had football workouts starting weeks before everyone else had to go back to school. It was very hard to leave someone who you consistently hung out with everyday but we knew this day was going to come. Although knowing he had to leave that next day we made sure we kept in touch. With Austin leaving for college I also had to get prepared to leave for school myself.

Reflecting back on the first night I spent at Averett it was an orientation visit and during the day we would tour the campus in groups and do activities throughout the day. I can remember the the first game we played and I got lucky to say the least. I'm not a big public speaker so when we did any type of group of group activities I kinda shied away in the back of the crowd. The game consisted of blow pops and depending on how many letters were in the name of that flavor, you had to counteract with interesting things about you. For example, if you had the blow pop that was "apple" you would have to name five interesting facts about yourself. However if you picked one like "Strawberry" then you were out of luck. I remember picking apple and I yelled "yes!" But I said it louder than I thought I did and my tour guide mentor kinda chuckled over my sigh of relief. After we were done with the group games and touring the campus, we were finally able to go back to our rooms for the night and unpack. Even though I knew that I was only spending one night I was still a little nervous about who was going to be my roommate. Once I got back to my room I met my roommate for the night and he seemed really cool, I had nothing to worry about.

Well as the night went on there was no chance of me getting any sleep. Everyone at the orientation was all put in the same area with one another, there a lobby in front of my room and everybody filled the space dancing and carrying on to music. Once I came to realize that sleep was not a factor I decided to meet up with some of the lacrosse guys I met earlier that day on our tours. As I hooked up with we all hung out in one room and talked about our high school lacrosse teams and where everyone was from. It was nice getting to know the guys a little bit more to get a better relationship with them from the very beginning.

As the night carried on into the morning, I managed to get a little sleep before heading back home. When I got everything packed up in the car my parents quickly asked me how was the night and all I could spit out before crashing in the back seat was "It was good." But, in my mind it was more than good because after my orientation I felt better about going to Averett. I think what gave me a positive vibe about it all was the people I met that night and how outgoing they were to meet me. It was a whole new atmosphere than my high school and I was starting to like that change.

During that summer, it was pretty busy from when I got back from my orientation. I was beginning to start shopping for things for college like, shelves, carpet, tv, e.t.c. With the business of shopping, I was also in the process of getting in contact with my roommate. I wanted to room with someone from the lacrosse team, but it didn't work out that for me. I got roomed with a baseball player named Alex. I was completely nervous about having a roommate because with being an only child I never actually experienced having someone else living with me. I messaged Alex one day on instagram, firstly making sure it was the right Alex and secondly wondering what he was going to bring to the room- so we wouldn't be bringing double the amount of stuff. I didn't know if I was going to like Alex or not, but I really enjoyed being around him. We continued to text off and on all the way up to the day we were moving in. I arrived at Averett before him and we started bringing things to the room and started to unpack. I was so nervous about meeting Alex and his family in person, not knowing how to react around him. As we were finishing the last little bit of items of my stuff, my family and I heard a knock on the door, it was time to meet my roommate.

I opened the door and I saw him first with a handful of stuff in his hands and his family and girlfriend following right behind him. Alex and I both said "hey" and we continued to help each other to get the room how we wanted it to be. Once we both got unpacked my family and his hit it off from the very beginning and I was starting to feel a sense of relief knowing that God had placed me with a good person to live with.

I found him to be extremely funny and a outgoing person. He would always play music and sing along with it sometimes being funny about or just casually singing. We would stay up hours into the night watching "Impractical Jokers" laughing our heads off. Having Alex around eased the pain of being away from home because the day my parents left me, it was very hard to say goodbye to them. With the help of him keeping my mind off of things I was able to do just fine on my own. I can honestly say that our room was probably one of the best rooms on our hall but the only downfall was that we couldn't control the AC. So some days we would walk into the room and start instantly sweating because it was so hot.

One day after I got out of class, it was still early into the first semester so the weather was still warm and as I was walked into the room, I saw Alex standing in front of one of our fans with his pants down with just his underwear on. It was a funny sight to see but I could understand his struggle with possibly having a heat stroke.

Along with having Alex as a friend I also spent time with some of the lacrosse players and see what they were up to. Although I didn't spend much time with them due my classes starting up and from the very beginning they were no joke. I knew that it was going to be a rough semester if I didn't get any help so I asked around to see if I could get tutors and everybody that I talked to recommended me to talk to a young man named Andruw. Everyone had nothing but high praise about this guy saying he's very helpful and extremely smart. On top of that he is majoring in nursing as well. A couple of days went by and my grandma told me to check my mailbox because she had sent me a letter, as I was walking down to the mailroom I saw Andruw and I recognized him from our orientation as he was one of the orientation leaders. So at first I was kinda skeptical about talking to him not knowing what to say other than "I need your help." I walked over to him and said "Hey, it's Andruw right?" He responded back and told me that it was him indeed and so I went on to explain my dilemma to him about my classes. The cool thing he told me was is that he took most of my classes already because he is a nursing major as well. He went on to say that he would be more than glad to help me in any way he can. From there on out we grew a pretty tight knit friendship with each other throughout my first year of college. At the beginning of college it was a new atmosphere for me, meaning all the new people I met and transitioning to another school which was also in another state. The one transition that I enjoyed the most was my class schedule and how close I was to my classes. Some days I would only have two classes and other days I would have three. In high school I was getting up around 6:30 every morning so I would make to school on time at 8:00. Some of college classes wouldn't even start until noon. Even if I had an early class I could stay in bed longer knowing that my classes were only a walking distance away from my dorm room. I remembered the first day I had my math class and on the door it said class was canceled. It was bittersweet knowing I didn't have class but sucked that I got up for nothing. During my first semester, there was one class sucked the most for me and that was chemistry. There was two parts to the class, as in a lecture section and a lab section which the lecture wasn't the bad part however the lab put me through a whirlwind. As you walked into lab you would see everything you needed laid out on the tables and the assignment on the board. The lab consisted of what we did in lecture that day and so when I saw the lab on the board I asked why we were learning a new chapter. He responded back saying "we learned this today in class." So that pretty much sums up how that class went for me. Most of the time I would grab someone in the class ask them if they could help guide me through the assignment and luckily they said yes.

That day as the class was putting the lab equipment away I was carrying our groups beaker and right before I had set it down I bumped my elbow on the countertop and drop the beaker on the floor and just watched it shattered into a million pieces. As in embarrassed as I was and already having a bad day in that class, my professor laughed it off and told me everything was alright and that definitely made me feel better. Although this wasn't the first time he had to worry about me, while also messing with the bunsen burner I could never get it to light until one day I was messing with it and the flame ignited into the air and almost caught me on fire. I was lucky to come out okay however I was missing a few hairs on my knuckles. Along with going through day to day experience in college, the team and I were starting our team workouts during the off-season. Since we couldn't do much during the off season, our practices consisted of a lot of conditioning and speed and agility drills. It was a much more different atmosphere than my high school workouts. They were much more intense and it didn't help that it was at pretty hot outside. On Saturday mornings we would do speed and agility on the game field. During our speed and agility workouts we would work on the fundamentals of cutting and explosion using cone drills, ladder drills, and focusing on our dynamic warm ups. At the very end of our practice we would have to do conditioning. That consisted on us starting at the field goal post and we had to run to the other field goal post in a certain amount of time. One time I remember we did that sprint 10 times before our coach whistled us in to end practice. Even though it was tough at times I definitely had a blast playing this sport and what made it better was the guys I was playing with.

CHAPTER 11

Psalm 37:24

As the first semester was slowly fading and the second semester just arising, I was coming to a point of questioning my major. After going through my first semester of college I was coming to realize that I didn't necessarily want to go into nursing anymore, I didn't feel like it was the right fit for me. After talking to Andruw about nursing and what he was doing during his clinicals, it opened my eyes and made me realize that maybe nursing wasn't for me. I felt so lost at the time knowing I was paying all this money to go to a college when I didn't even know what I wanted my major to be. During high school I thought I had everything figured out by my senior year and everything was looking up for me. It was the first time I actually felt like I was somewhat adulting on my own and I could honestly say it was a great feeling knowing I was on top of things. Once I arrived in college, that's where I finally got the chance to dig in and learn more about my major, it was more of a learning experience for me as I went through my freshman year of college. I was at the point of taking my anger out on Andruw because I felt like I was at this point wasting my life away. One night as we were hanging out in his dorm room we were looking at majors that our University offered and one thing that caught me and Andruw's eye was Medical Technology. As we looked into the description on what the major is about we saw that it was basically dealing with lab work just like Lab Corp. I also saw that I would only go to school for three years and work my senior year in college and sadly at that point I wasn't looking at the big picture and I jumped into this new major, panicked and all only because I wouldn't have to go to school my senior year. Later on down the road, once the second semester began my class schedule was geared towards lab work for this new major. I remember pumping myself up, convincing myself that this is the career for me. Once I started these classes, once again the lecture portion of the class was perfectly fine it was just the lab part that took me for surprise. This class of mine was Microbiology and all we did in lab was practice the proper way to use test tubes, microscopes, and how to handle unknown bacteria. At first I really enjoyed lab and I actually believed that I was going to stick with this major for a long time career. As I was thinking that my life was going great and I felt in control again, something struck my mind one morning about this new major. As I was getting ready for class I kept thinking to myself is this really something I want to do for the rest of my life? I then started to picture myself years later down the road imaging me working as a lab technician and all I could see was a negative outcome. I was picturing me not enjoying going to work and not enjoying the work itself. After those thoughts ran through my head, my classes were never the same again. Every time I would enter lab I would get a sour feeling as in I didn't enjoy it and I didnt see the fun in it anymore. I knew at that point that if I wasn't able to enjoy it for that short amount time I've been in that class, who's to say that I would enjoy this career for several years from now? With struggling with my academic career choice, lacrosse was becoming a struggle for me as well. It wasn't becoming a struggle because of the sport itself but when you're a student athlete your time to fit in education and sports is a difficult task to do. As I didnt know what I wanted to do for my career I also had to focus on lacrosse and our practices. Some days we wouldn't get back from a road game until midnight and we would have class the next morning. Sure, it is our choice to play, but after a while it takes a toll on your life. I started to feel like everything was pilling up on top on me and my grades were starting to reflect that, just like they have in the past. It was getting to the point where I would be so tired from a previous game or a late night practice and I didnt have enough willpower to do any work once I got back to my room. At that point I had to make a decision that I didn't necessarily want to do and that was to drop lacrosse. It was so hard to leave the guys on the team that I grew a tight relationship with but this decision had to be done. I always told myself and my mom as well that my grades come first before any sport I play. I finally made the decision to devote my life towards my school work and to figure out what I wanted to do major wise. Later in the month, I took a visit back home one weekend to see my parents and girlfriend. Earlier that week I was texting my dad asking him about different career paths and even having a mental breakdown over the phone, we mentioned many things in the rescue force because I knew for sure that I wanted to do something medical. Seeing my dad and talking with him that weekend was the big factor why I wanted to come home. My dad did everything from being a fireman, Duke Life Flight paramedic, rescue scuba diver, and he even raced late model race cars. My mom always told me that she was a nervous wreck while dating my dad. Knowing that he picked some of the most dangerous jobs to pursue, but that's what made my dad happy and I wanted to feel that happiness he felt while working. My dad always stressed to me the importance of enjoying what you do because if you're not enjoying it then you're just wasting your time. As I arrived at my house Saturday morning I was quickly greeted by my two dogs Sadie and Goliath jumping all over me very excited to see me walk through the door. My dad was just finishing up breakfast for my mom but he stopped immediately and made me two scrambled eggs, hashbrowns, and bacon. On the other side of the kitchen my mom was making me a fresh batch of coffee just for me. Without hesitation I jumped into the conversation about my major and or career choice. I always had thoughts growing up of becoming a fireman and captain just like my old man but he immediately shut that down real quick. At first I was a little annoyed that he didn't let me finish but there was no need after explaining his life as a former fireman and how dangerous that job was. I respected his opinion very much but I still kept that career open in my mind. Hours went by still talking about this matter and all of the sudden a light bulb went off in my head and I thought about paramedics. My parents, especially my dad, were pretty enthusiastic about that idea, sure it was another dangerous job but my parents and I thought that it would be a great career path for me. When looking at a future job I always wanted to be able to help others, be active, and somehow be related to the medical field and give back to the men and women who saved my life. I felt like paramedics was a good fit for me, with deciding on taking on my new career path, I had to once again make a difficult decision by leaving my school and friends. My first roommate left after the first semester so Andruw was able to room with me during the second semester and we became very close friends with each other. I had to finally tell Andruw that I wasn't rooming with him in the fall and that I was transferring to a different school. Not only leaving him but all my other friends that I became very close to. I knew that I had to do what was best for me even though I knew it would come with some side effects, so at that moment of telling everyone my plans I made the most out of my final spring semester and I will always keep those memories I made at school in a special place in my heart.

CHAPTER 12

Deuteronomy 31:6

Waking up in my college dorm for the last time was kinda bitter sweet knowing that it was the end of the semester but also keeping in mind that I was going to leave a lot of good friends behind. Before leaving however, I took the time to load up my final belongings and then stayed the afternoon to eat lunch with them. After we ate lunch we visited our local coffee shop on campus, trying to use up our final "Jut bucks" that we had remaining on our card. It was funny because a lot of them had only a few dollars left on their card and could only buy but so much in their store. On the other hand, I still had about twenty dollars left on my card and I was trying to buy everything thing I could to use up all that money. Ranging from airheads, soft drinks, and I even offered to pay for someone else's items. Leaving the coffee shop it looked like we had raided the store with all the mismatched items we were coming out with. As we sat outside with our Slim Jim's and Coca Cola's we basically talked about the next semester and everyone's plans for the upcoming summer. We had a great last talk and of course we had to take group pictures to cap off a great school year. after telling everyone goodbye and I sat in my car, it was crazy to believe that my first year of college was officially over.

My friends from back home must have known that I was coming home that day because my phone was ringing every minute while I was trying to drive. I was talking to them over the phone as I was driving back and right away we were trying to make plans to kick off the summer. Once I got home, it took me a little while to get everything unpacked out of my car, because all I wanted to do was go see my friends and hang out with them like old times. We had a lot to catch up on so needless to say my car car didn't get fully unpacked until three weeks later after I came back home. My summer was starting off great as my friend Michael took me out to go bowling and play some pool. Being the competitive people we are, we tried to beat each other in every game we played. Getting more excited than the kids beside us bowling. But it felt great to feel like we were twelve again and not focus on our worries but just to have fun and enjoy life. Shortly after, my other friend Austin took me to Lake Eno and we swam for a little while, well I take that back Austin couldn't swim so he was glued to the edge of the lake not letting go of a nearby log he used as a floaty. All in all the summer was starting off to a great start as it was good to finally reconnect and put our worries aside for the time being.

The good times paused for a little while as my girlfriend and I broke up this summer and I'll have to admit it was rough at times but I felt like this break up brought me closer to God. That might sound weird but after asking God for help in this situation and also having my closet friends by my side it numbed the pain and made it seem like it was all just a bad dream. Shortly after the break up, my parents and I went to church that Sunday and to be totally honest I was not in the mood to go, but my parents insisted that I did. As we arrived we walked into the church and were greeted by everyone standing at the door. Soon after we found my aunt and uncle who goes to church there as well, we all took a seat in the sanctuary and chatted with them before the service began. In front of me I noticed the youth pastor, Alex Miles as he was talking to some other people but then he noticed me and came over to where I was seated and began to talk to me. Alex is an important part in my life as we was there for me during my thyroid surgery and lead us in prayer before I was put under. So fast forwarding to the moment when Alex talked to me at church, he shook my hand and sat down next to me and asked how school was going. I told him that I just got out for the summer and that I had different plans, of course he asked what were those plans and I told him I wanted to pursue a career as a paramedic. Kinda skeptical about his response, he replied back by saying how his former roommate did the same thing and though that was a great idea for me. That definitely made me feel good about myself knowing I had someone like him backing up my future goals. After talking a little bit more he told me that he was actually preaching this Sunday instead of the actual pastor. I always liked when Alex would lead the service because I felt like he was closer to my age group and we could relate to each more easily. If the music they sang wasn't powerful enough, Alex surely made the message hit home for me. The whole time he was preaching it felt like he was speaking to me, talking about struggles in life and having to adapt to these certain obstacles to make it feasible to maintain a healthy spiritual life. Alex, at the end of his sermon asked the audience to bow their heads and close their eyes in prayer. As Alex was praying I said a little prayer to myself and asked God for wisdom and guidance as I pursue my future and make it a mission to allow God to come first in any decision I make. I remember for the first time in my life I was crying my eyes out in church, but it wasn't because I was sad however I was happy and it felt so good to just cry. Knowing that God will take care of me no matter how big the circumstance is, there is no greater obstacle in this world that he can't handle. After getting done with prayer, it had lit a fire underneath of me that was so full of enlightenment and motivation that I felt way better than I did when I walked into church that morning. After that Sunday, it seemed like doors were opening for me. After flipping back and forth about what career path I should take, I fell into being a paramedic. Well at first I wanted to go into the fire department like my Dad when he was younger but he recommended me to go into EMT school and later on become a paramedic. We talked for a long time about this career because this part of the medical field can see some horrific stuff. But, still knowing the circumstances I still wanted to give it a try. With my Dad being involved with Duke Life Flight and the fire department, I wanted to follow into his footsteps. When class started this summer, my biggest fear was that there was going to be a lot of people in my class. Walking into the class on the first day I was pretty happy to see that it wasn't a big class. However on the other hand I was nervous about having to make new friends and I even wondered to myself if anyone would talk to me. A couple of guys rolled in pretty soon after me and they were very cool. Out of all the students I did know one person that was apart of the Elon Academy program with me. It became a dream come true for me because me and all of the guys instantly became friends. The first week was thrown at us so quick with a lot of information and notes, it all started to become overwhelming at times. However there were times where we would have to run scenarios and act like they were real calls. There has been disco ball parties all the way to a motor vehicle collision where we actually put some of dummy's in our trucks. We had an old ambulance that the EMT and paramedics class were able to use and we would drive up in our ambulance and react to whatever call was given to us. This was very fun at times but also very stressful. We had tests to take, not just written tests but scenario and skills based tests. Along with taking written tests we had to be able to perform in a single and double man rescue. We had to be able to determine what the problem was and how to treat it, whether that may be splinting, bleeding control, medication administration, all the way to delivering a baby. They were pass or fail and no in between. Throughout the course there were a series of three scenario based tests plus the written exam before you could even take the state test. There were many of those where I would doubt myself before beginning the test to the point where I would be pacing the floor back and forth before it was my turn to go. It was definitely harder than I expected going into this class which made me study harder than I ever have for any class that i've took in the past. I made it and passed all of my test prior to the final, some harder than others but I made it and it gave me a little confidence booster going into the final. The day before the finals I had a ride along with our local EMS, and that was definitely an experience in itself. There were calls that day where I couldn't even imagine if I didn't see it with my own eyes. With all the craziness I had endured, I felt like I was ready for anything thrown my way on test day. Waking up on finals day, I surprisingly wasn't that nervous. I started my normal routine by waking up after my sixth alarm went off, got cleaned up and dressed in my uniform. Before walking out the door my parents stopped me before I walked and told me they wanted to say a quick prayer with me. I feel like they sensed the nervousness in me knowing that my career of being a paramedic was on the line. Some of the guys showed up early to be one of the first ones to go. When first arriving on campus, they still haven't begun and they were waiting and watching the classroom door to see if an instructor was going to signal someone into the testing room. With me arriving later than most of my classmates I was one of the last ones to go, and when my time came all of my nerves hit me all at once. All of my classmates who went before passed their final so it put a lot of pressure on me to do good. As I was signaled into the testing area, the instructor said "now, before you start take a deep breath and relax". Yeah, that advice didnt help me at all and my nerves were all tore up. I couldn't think straight and everything I had ever learned in this class was gone, my mind went into total darkness. When given my scenario I quickly tried to remember the things off the top of my head and work my way up from there. Long story short without going into detail is that my patient lived but I hit one critical fail that made me fail the scenario and ended up failing the course. After talking with my professors I left the room but didn't want to go back into the first room where all of my friends were sitting and waiting for me to come back. I stayed in the bathroom for a little while to collect myself before I confronted them. Not saying a word to them being that I was frustrated and embarrassed, I wanted to grab my things and leave as quickly as possible. At this point, college classes has already begun and my time to even think about enrolling into classes were too late. I did have thoughts about taking the longer EMT course and retake the class, but then I thought was it a sign from God? Like is this not the path he wants me to take? I had plenty of friends and family tell me I should retake the course but deep down inside I didn't enjoy it the first time. As time progressed through the class i've grown to realize that that part of the medical field wasn't for me. With me being a first time college Student in my family, I promised my Mom and Dad that I would graduate with a four year college degree. From that moment forward I believed God had laid it on my heart to go back to school in the spring and finish what I had started. With being out of school until January I needed a job, with bouncing back and forth finding a decent paying job I ended up getting a job where my Dad works delivering doors and windows. My Dad had already warned me about the difficulty of this job and how exhausting it can be. At this point however I just wanted a job. Already there has been days that have been really hot and really cold and a lot of hard labor. Although this job was hard at times, it makes me realize how much more I appreciate and want to go back to school. I had older gentlemen who worked in the office at work asking me "so you're going back to school right?", a lot of the guys seen potential in me to do more with my life and told me that they too wanted to see me graduate. With me working and taking this time off from school, has really helped me find my craft and what I really want in school and life itself.

My plan is to go back to school, graduate with a bachelor's degree in Biology and then go on to graduate school to further my career into Oncology. I know becoming a doctor is really hard to do and a major sacrifice timewise. But at the end of the day, if I can be a help to someone who is battling cancer and somehow make an impact on someone's life then all the struggle that comes with it will all be worth it. As I begin to start a new chapter in my life, I can't help but thank my closest family and friends and most importantly God, without them I wouldn't of known what I am actually capable of doing.

Along with the love and support from all of them, writing this book helped me emotionally and spiritually to get out of dark places in my life. I felt like bottling up my emotions about my life story but ever since I began to speak about it, everyone has come to me and said that I needed to share my story. I wasn't too sure if I should at first because there was some rough patches in my life that I didn't feel comfortable talking about. Although, I came to realize that I needed to share my story, not to help myself necessarily but help others who have been following my path and or who are struggling with life in general. I prayed long and hard about this, not knowing where to begin and never writing a book in my life I knew it was going to be a difficult task in itself but knowing that they're people who may have the same struggles or even different struggles, gave me so much motivation to write this book and hopefully lead others not into evil but into the hands of the Lord.

Throughout my time on earth, I've learned many things about myself. Honestly, learned more these past five years than any other time in my life. People can call me crazy or stupid when I say this; but, I'm glad I had cancer and I'm glad I tore my ACL. The reason behind this is because without those two big things happening in my life, I would have never known how strong I really am as a person- mentally and physically. I am forever thankful for being able to live to see another day; and I've learned to never take God's creation for granted, because it can be easily taken away from you. If you're struggling with some hard times right now- whether it's with your marriage, relationship, a relative passing, financial issues- I want you to know that those things are basically speed bumps. Whenever something good may be happening and then a speed bump comes around, how are you going to deal with that adversity? Are you going to run away from your issues? For everyone that is having troubles in his or her life, I want you to know that you're not alone, because I'm fighting in your corner with you. There have been many times that I have felt alone and helpless; so, I want to be that person to help you up when you fall down. As I said earlier, make sure you have goals in life to help you move forward and to keep you going everyday. If you always look at the bad things in life and never glance at the good things, then all you are doing is slowing yourself down from living life. This world God created is a blessing to us and we need to live our lives to the fullest and never ever hold back our dreams and what we believe in. Make sure you're doing the things you love in life and stop worrying about other people's opinion or others who say you can't do something. How does the person next to you know what you can or can't do? If you want something bad enough then go chase it and never look back. Writing this story isn't really for me, I want it to be motivation to my readers and the community around me and all over the world. I share my story because a lot of people don't believe that God is working 24/7 and many think that he doesn't really exist. Well, let me tell you this God didn't give me or my uncle cancer. He cured mine and he also didn't want to see my uncle suffer know more so he took his son to heaven. Trust me, if I could ask my uncle right now if he had an option to come back to earth would he do it? And I bet you he would say heck no! There are a lot of famous athletes that have written some books themselves telling their stories, but I feel like a lot of people are intimidated by those kind of books, not because they're bad readers, but because they feel like they can't connect with them. I want to make it clear that I'm thinking about you and praying about you because I know what hard times feels like and I never want to wish that on anyone. Make sure you live life to the fullest and go for your dreams even if there might be a speed bump along the way. Cancer did not defeat me; it only made me stronger mentally, physically, and religiously and I couldn't have been more blessed to have cancer because it has made me to who I am today. I've learned a whole new definition to being brave and lionhearted that nobody can understand but me. However, what we all can understand is that our troubles, worries, or problems in life are just speed bumps and we can get over them.

Printed in the United States
By Bookmasters